The Boy Who Gave His Lunch Away

JOHN 6:1-15 FOR CHILDREN

Written by
Dave Hill

Illustrated by
Betty Wind

CH Books

1967 CONCORDIA PUBLISHING HOUSE, ST. LOUIS, MISSOURI

MANUFACTURED IN THE UNITED STATES OF AMERICA
RIGHTS RESERVED
N 0-570-06027-3

Joel lived a happy life
down by Lake Galilee.
"We have a farm," he liked to say,
"for Mom and Dad and me."

His dad grew barley, oats, and wheat
for baking rolls and bread.
"What we don't eat we give away,"
was what he always said.

Joel knew what Father meant,
for EVERYONE needs bread.
"But why are some folks poor," he asked,
"when we are so well fed?"

"It isn't fair at all, I know,
but someday," Father said,
"the good Messiah will be here,
and He will be our King.
Then there will be no rich or poor.
We'll all have everything!"

So Joel helped his folks at work.
He rose each day at four
and washed the pots and scrubbed the pans
and swept and mopped the floor.
He helped his dad fill up the bags
of bread to give the poor.

One warm June day a neighbor stopped
to buy a loaf of bread.
"I'm on my way to see the King.
He's right nearby," he said.

"A king?" said Joel.
"Right nearby?
You must be fooling me!"
The stranger shook his head.
"I'm not!
Why, people say that He
is God's Messiah — here at last!
Why don't you come and see?"

"Is this the man named Jesus, sir?"
asked Father with a smile.
"Because, if so, my son can go
and see Him for a while."

"The very man!" the neighbor cried.
"You've heard of Him, I see!"

"I've heard He's kind and loves the Lord.
That's good enough for me!"

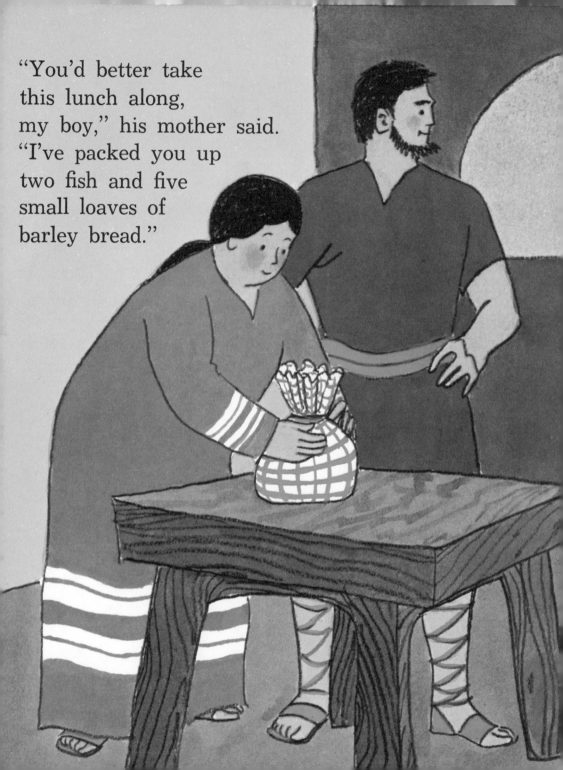

"You'd better take this lunch along, my boy," his mother said. "I've packed you up two fish and five small loaves of barley bread."

"I won't need that!"
cried Joel. "Why,
the King will
feed the poor!"

But Father told him, "Take it, son,"
as they went out the door.

So up the road, with l[...]
the two went with a s[...]
They soon came to a r[...]
stretched out for half a[...]
"He must be near! We [...]
in just a little while!"

in hand,

crowd

the King

"That's Jesus there!"
a voice called out,
and Joel turned to see.
There stood a man
as plain and poor
as any man could be!

He ran up close
where he could see,
and hear what Jesus said.
"Is this the King –
this plain, poor man?
I'm glad I brought
some bread!"

Then Jesus spoke; His voice was strong:
"Bring all the sick to Me!"
And Joel stared as lame folks walked
and blind men cried: "I see!"

As Joel watched, he saw the sick
made whole and well and strong.
"Our King! Our King!" a shout rose up
from all who came along.

Then Jesus turned
and raised a hand
and spoke out
loud and clear:
"The kingdom that
God promised you
you see
already here!

"The kingdom
the Messiah brings
is full of
love and joy.
It's like a happy
dinner that
a king gives
for his boy."

The day grew short, and someone cried:
"I wish we had some bread!"
A man beside the Teacher spoke:
"How will these folks be fed?"

When Joel heard, he ran right up:
"I have some bread and fish.
I'll gladly share them with the crowd
if that is what you wish!"

"Five loaves? Two fish? For all this mob?"
asked one man with a frown.
But Jesus took the food and said,
"Have everyone sit down."

"We thank you, Father," Jesus prayed
and blessed and broke the bread.
Then His disciples passed it out
till ALL THE CROWD was fed.

"A miracle!" somebody cried.
"There's food for all to share!"
The helpers even gathered up
twelve baskets full to spare.

"Hooray! Hooray!" the people cheered.
"Shall we crown Jesus king?
He'll always give us what we need,
and we'll have everything!"
But Jesus turned and hurried off.
He wanted no such thing!

DEAR PARENTS:

Like Joel, people in New Testament times looked for the promised Messiah to come and establish His kingdom. In their deep longing they hoped for a time when the hungry would have enough to eat and the poor would have all their needs supplied.

In Jesus, the Messiah, the kingdom of God came according to promise. Jesus announced the Kingdom in words: "The time is fulfilled, and the kingdom of God is at hand" (Mark 1:15). He performed many signs to indicate the coming of God's kingdom, or gracious rule, over men. The feeding of the 5,000 with five loaves and two fishes is such a sign. This feeding miracle reminds us of parables in which Jesus compared the kingdom of God to a great dinner banquet. He invites all people, good and bad, rich and poor. God provides for the needs of people in generous abundance at this banquet. There is plenty for all, even when our faith is too small to see how God can provide. Resources at the banquet may be limited, but Christ uses them to feed the thousands who come to Him.

The people who were fed by the loaves and fishes were impressed by Jesus' powers. They wanted to make Him a bread king to satisfy their hunger and other needs of daily life. Because they misunderstood the King and His kingdom, "Jesus withdrew again to the hills by Himself" (John 6:15). He is more than a supplier of free bread. He is the "Bread of Life" (John 6:35), who brings the rule of God to us and gives us His goodness and love.

Will you help your child see the meaning of our story as the work of Christ putting God's kingdom into action? Will you help him experience the joy and abundance of life in Christ's church?

THE EDITOR